EDUCATOR'S
QUICK REFERENCE GUIDE

to growth mindsets

by Mary Cay Ricci

WHAT ARE MINDSETS?

Thanks to the research of Dr. Carol Dweck, Stanford University professor of psychology, society is going through a shift in thinking about learning and intelligence. Dweck (2006) described a belief system that asserts that intelligence, skills, and talents can be developed, and coined the term *growth mindset*.

FIXED MINDSET

Conversely, Dweck (2006) coined the term *fixed mindset*, which is a belief system in which one believes that intelligence, skills, and talent are something you are born with—they are genetic, and although everyone can learn new things, your innate level of intelligence cannot be changed. A person applying fixed mindset thinking might believe that he or she has predetermined intelligence, skills, or talents in a particular area, but not in other areas. A child or adult using a fixed mindset might believe that he or she will never be good in a particular subject or talent or be afraid to try something that he or she thinks is too difficult or at which he or she fears failure.

GROWTH MINDSET

Teachers and parents with a growth mindset believe that children can achieve at higher levels—with effort, perseverance, resiliency, and the right set of strategies. Learners with a growth mindset believe that they can grow their intelligence, skills, and talents with hard work and learn just about anything. It might take some struggle and mistakes along the way, but they understand that with resiliency and perseverance, they can grow and be successful.

CAN YOU *BE* A GROWTH MINDSET PERSON?

Contrary to what many believe, there really isn't anyone who is a growth mindset person or a fixed mindset person. The mindsets come into play based on the situation that you are in—you either believe that with perseverance, some mistakes along the way, and the right set of strategies you can achieve something, or you believe that you were not born with the capacity or ability to achieve in this particular area. We apply growth mindset thinking to some situations and apply fixed mindset thinking to other situations. As educators, the goal is to apply growth mindset thinking for yourselves as you learn new instructional approaches as well as with the children that you interact with.

FIXED VERSUS GROWTH MINDSET THINKING

Fixed Mindset	Growth Mindset
• Skills, talents, athletic ability, music/art ability, and intelligence are things we are born with—hereditary or genetic—and even though we can all learn new things, we will never be good at some things because we were not born with that talent. • Adults or children with a fixed mindset may give up easily and decide to check out of the learning process because they don't believe that they possess the ability to understand this particular new learning.	• Skills, talents, athletic ability, music/art ability, and intelligence are things we can learn with perseverance, resiliency, work ethic, and the right set of strategies. • An adult or child with a growth mindset perseveres even in the face of barriers.

4 COMPONENTS OF A GROWTH MINDSET LEARNING ENVIRONMENT

There are four components that are essential to a growth mindset learning culture (Ricci, 2015; see **Figure 1**). These are areas that each learning environment should strive to obtain. These cannot happen overnight and sometimes not even within one school year. These actions should be a long-term commitment, and educators must have a growth mindset themselves in order to persevere to attain these goals.

FIGURE 1. **4 components.** From Ricci, 2017.

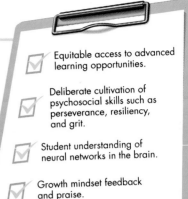

- ☑ Equitable access to advanced learning opportunities.
- ☑ Deliberate cultivation of psychosocial skills such as perseverance, resiliency, and grit.
- ☑ Student understanding of neural networks in the brain.
- ☑ Growth mindset feedback and praise.

EQUITABLE ACCESS TO ADVANCED LEARNING

Do all of the students in your class, school, or district have access to enriched and accelerated learning? Is a label (such as **"gifted"**), a grade, or a specific test score a requirement to access these opportunities? Ongoing informal assessment and observation should allow for all students, not just those with already developed abilities, to have access to and participate in advanced learning opportunities. This may be teacher-facilitated small-group work within the classroom or an advanced class offering at the secondary level.

Teachers must have a growth mindset in order to allow this to happen. No gatekeeping, no barriers, no "sorry, but you are not 'ready' for this." Once students have this access, are supports or scaffolds put in place to help students succeed? "Sink or swim" beliefs have no place in the education of our young students.

GROWTH MINDSET PRAISE AND FEEDBACK

Provide praise and feedback based on what a child *does*, not who they are. Instead of saying "You are so smart!" say things like "I can see you put forth a lot of effort!" Continuing to tell children that they are "smart" can cause them to become risk-averse, which can translate to always wanting to take the easy way so that they continue to look smart no matter what. Strive for a learning space that praises effort, struggle, and perseverance. Provide feedback and praise when students select difficult tasks to conquer or try new strategies when learning a concept. This feedback also encompasses how you react to students' academic performance, such as a typically strong student not having success on an assessment.

Fixed Mindset Statement:
You are so smart!
Growth Mindset Replacement Statement:
I can see how much effort you put into your work!

You made several mistakes on this assignment.
Mistakes help us learn . . . now let's figure out what went wrong and approach it again in a new way.

Some people are just not "math" people.
Just because math is challenging for you right now doesn't mean that you can't master it. It may take some time, but you will get it.

You are so lucky; you don't have to study much!
It seems like this came easily for you. Maybe we can find something more challenging for you to try.

LEAVE ROOM FOR "YET"

The learning environment, whether it is a classroom, field, court, in front of a piano, or at the kitchen table, should be a setting where both adults and students favor the word **"yet."**

> ❝ You are not quite there . . . yet . . . with more practice, you will be. ❞

Keep the power of the word **"yet"** in mind as you speak to your students as well as for yourself, "You haven't quite reached that student, *yet*." Yet is a word that communicates hope and the belief that understanding will eventually happen.

DELIBERATE CULTIVATION OF PSYCHOSOCIAL SKILLS

The cultivation of noncognitive/psychosocial skills is imperative, for both the students who have not yet developed their abilities, skills, and talents and high-performing students. The most important skills that must be deliberately modeled, taught, and cultivated are *perseverance* and *resiliency*.

Development of these psychosocial skills should be part of the climate of the classroom, discussed across every content area and modeled daily by the entire class or school community. Students can self-evaluate and make plans for improving and tracking their growth in these skills; then they can make a conscious effort to improve their ability to bounce back after a less-than-successful performance or failure to master a new concept. They can begin working toward being diligent about their actions. Hand-in-hand with nurturing perseverance and resiliency is teaching students how to learn from errors and failure. Mistakes can be considered "data"—this data can help a student set goals for moving toward success.

We know that some of our students may demonstrate resiliency outside of school—perhaps they go home to a stressful household or live in a neighborhood that requires resilient behaviors. The kind of resiliency that may be demonstrated outside of school does not easily translate into the kind of resiliency needed in school. Academic resiliency is what we strive for—that ability to bounce back from setbacks that may occur in the learning process.

The First Step to Cultivating Psychosocial Skills

A recommended first step in deliberate cultivation of psychosocial skills is to reflect upon what is already in place in your classroom or school. At first, focus on noncognitive skills that overlap, such as:

perseverance	resiliency	grit

Then, gather some interested staff members. Together, brainstorm school- or districtwide experiences that will deliberately cultivate these noncognitive factors. Build the concept of resiliency and perseverance with students. What are some examples of resiliency . . . nonexamples? What does resiliency look like in the classroom . . . in sports . . . in the arts? What historical figures, scientists, and/or literary characters demonstrate resiliency?

A CONCEPTUAL UNDERSTANDING OF NEURAL NETWORKS

Neuroscience has had a significant impact on teaching and learning. Recent brain research negates the notion that intelligence is **"fixed"** from birth. Both formal and informal studies demonstrate that the brain can develop with the proper stimulus. Other current research in neuroscience emphasizes the concept of *neuroplasticity*.

What Is Neuroplasticity?

Through lack of experiences or practice, neuroplasticity in our brain eliminates or weakens connections. The neural connections may go unused for the children whose families cannot provide academic experiences or intellectual stimuli during the summer, while the students who are provided with such opportunities during the summer can maintain their learning.

> *Neuroplasticity* is the ability of the brain to change, adapt, and "rewire" itself throughout our entire lives.

WHY LEARN ABOUT THE BRAIN?

We now know so much more about the brain that it cannot help but inform the way we approach learning, instruction, and motivation. It is when educators and children (as well as their parents) learn about the brain and all of its potential and when they witness the impact that it has on learning that mindsets can begin to shift.

Cognitive ability tests measure developed ability. Therefore, if a child has never had an opportunity to develop the kinds of reasoning processes that these assessments measure, the outcome of one of these assessments would not be significant. David Lohman (2002), professor of educational psychology at the University of Iowa and cocreator of the Cognitive Abilities Test **(CogAT)**, stated that abilities are developed through experiences "in school and outside of school" (para. 3). When parents and educators review these **"intelligence"** scores, assumptions may be made about the child, and beliefs may kick in that place limits on the child's potential.

Having an understanding of neural networking can significantly increase motivation. In Carol Dweck's (2010) original New York City study, students reported that visualizing neural connections helped them move forward. In my visits to schools, I have often heard students state that they think about the neurons connecting when they are faced with a difficult task or have difficulty understanding a new skill or concept. This does not require going deep into neuroscience; just building a conceptual understanding can increase motivation to succeed.

How to Teach Students About the Brain

Teachers often think that they don't have time to teach students about their brains due to time constraints and an already overpacked curriculum. At the middle and high school level, this can be done in science or health classes. At all levels, it can be done through reading nonfiction texts about the brain (e.g., for our elementary-age students, I like *Your Fantastic Elastic Brain: Stretch It, Shape It* by JoAnn Deak). All that students really need to understand and conceptualize is the neural networking that takes place when we learn something new, practice it, and then master it.

MAKE MISTAKES AND FAILURE AN IMPORTANT PART OF LEARNING

Learning to embrace failure is hardly easy; however, once again, if students learn more about their brains and how they work, failure is accepted as just a normal part of the learning process. Students who internalize the understanding of the plasticity of the brain and the functional changes in the brain that occur when we learn can deal more constructively with setbacks. They are sometimes even more motivated to work toward mastery and will persist and persevere until they do.

Educators who value the importance of providing challenging opportunities for students find that students react to the challenge in different ways. Some students have a "Bring it on!" approach and embrace the challenge with enthusiasm. These students realize that they may not be successful and might even fail at a task or two, but want to take the risk and stretch themselves. Other students feel threatened by the challenge, are afraid they will not succeed, and will often give up before they put much effort into it.

CHANGING THE CLASSROOM CLIMATE

It is imperative that teachers develop a climate in their classrooms where failure is viewed as an expected and very important part of the learning process and students learn to reflect and redirect so that they can approach a challenging task in a new way or with more effort. Teachers can model this behavior themselves in the classroom.

8 Educator Tips About Mistakes and Failure

1
Share some of your best, most epic mistakes, then share what you learned from them.

2
Let students know that failure is their friend—it is an important part of learning.

3
Discuss the positive aspect of mistakes and failure every day. View errors and failures as **"data."**

4
When introducing a new skill or concept:
- Let students know that you welcome mistakes, and encourage students to share the errors with everyone so that everyone can learn from them.
- Let students know that you expect that there will be some struggle as they learn new things, which is great because struggle helps make new neural connections and builds resiliency!

5
Create a safe environment where no one makes fun of or comments on someone else's error in a negative way.

6
Encourage students to share some of their **"best"** or **"epic"** errors and what they learned from them.

7
Keep expectations high and let students know when they have not met those expectations, then tell them what they need to do to improve. Give them the time to redo the work and offer support in the process.

8
Circle errors on papers. Let students know that this means, "Look at this again." Provide feedback to them in writing or in person about the errors. Allow redos.

> " I can accept failure, everyone fails at something. But I can't accept not trying. "
> *Michael Jordan*

GRADES AND REDOS

Grades are not growth mindset friendly. Why? Because grades often emphasize the end result, not the process or the perseverance. Grades suggest where a student is at one moment of time in one particular subject in one particular skill or concept. Grades can also be subjective, especially in the early grades, and they do not predict a child's future, potential, or possibilities.

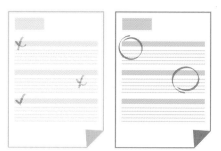

How to Grade

We need to use the act of grading a paper to build on the concept of learning from failure. For example, instead of putting an **"X"** next to an incorrect response, just circle the response. Let students know that whenever they see a circle on a paper that they have completed, it means "Look at this again" or "You don't quite get this yet." Then, provide the opportunity for them to reflect, revisit, and/or ask for clarification or reteaching of the concept.

GOAL-SETTING

One of the most important components in goal-setting is that we chose goals that focus on the journey instead of the end. In order to reach some goals, we must do something called *deliberate practice*. Not just regular old practice, but effective, deliberate practice. It is a specific kind of practice that is very planned and purposeful. The planning and purpose is focused on improving performance. It is not about just repeating something over and over without really thinking about it . . . the experience needs to be very focused on what is being practiced and why it needs to be practiced.

It is important to write down and plan for important goals. Take a look at this example from Joseph:

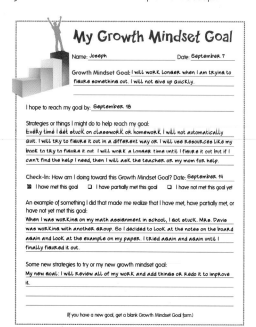

Let Students Reflect

A **"bad"** grade is an opportunity to reflect, regroup, and relearn. One of the biggest issues with grades is that some students work really, really hard for a B, C, or D . . . and others don't work that hard for an **A**. A hard-working, persistent student who earns a C may feel more motivated than a student who receives an **A** without a whole lot of effort. Some students are so busy trying to make the honor roll or get an **A** that they can lose their love of learning.

Let Students Try Again

If we really believe in the importance of learning from errors, we should allow students to redo assignments and retake assessments. A growth mindset educator will work with students and guide or help them to approach the learning in a new way. We also need to provide time and space for practice and feedback. Redoing assignments and retaking tests are both part of a growth mindset. After all, the goal is student learning, and by having an opportunity to reflect and relearn, a child can actually learn and understand the content. This is not, however, a good practice if nothing is in place to help students with the content between the original task and the task that is redone.

Say, for example, a math teacher allows students to retake an assessment within two weeks of taking it the first time. Sounds like a good practice until we find out that the math teacher does not provide opportunities for students to relearn the material. Afterschool sessions are a good time to invite students in who need to be taught the concept(s) again.

GET PARENTS INVOLVED

Information about growth and fixed mindsets, encouraging resilience, basic brain operations, and ways to praise their children are essential concepts that can be shared with parents.

In doing so, children will hear a consistent message from adults in their lives that will significantly contribute to developing and maintaining an "I can do this" attitude. This can be done by posting information on the school website, on social network sites, in newsletter blurbs, during principal coffee hours, and/or during a parent information evening.

Encourage Resilience

A central message to communicate with parents is *the importance of encouraging resilience* in their children. Parents often overlook opportunities for helping children learn to adjust to situations when they are faced with adversity or lack of success. This means children will eventually try to avoid anything where they are not very sure that they will be successful rather than view the situation as a challenge to arise to.

> **If a parent says to a child,** "No wonder you did not do well on that test; you are always playing video games," **or** "You shouldn't have tried out for that team in the first place; you knew it would be a long shot," **the parent is not contributing to building resilience.**

Form a Growth Mindset Committee

Form a growth mindset committee at school and invite a few parents to be part of it. Educators and parents can work together to plan communication and events that will help build a growth mindset school community. The parent organization at your school can form a book club and read *Mindsets for Parents: Strategies to Encourage Growth Mindsets in Kids* (2016). (This book includes book club questions as well, so school staff do not have to plan or be part of the group.)

Host a Growth Mindset Workshop

Invite parents and their children for a growth mindset workshop. At each table have reasoning games and/or puzzles that continually get more challenging. (ShapeOmetry, Chocolate Fix, Rush Hour, Brick by Brick are good reasoning games to use.) Just about every adult who participates will face challenge/failure/frustration—this provides the perfect opportunity to talk with parents about *what a growth mindset is* and *why it is important*.

Focus on the importance of struggle, failure, and mistakes:

1

Let parents know that the perseverance, tenacity, and application of strategies that are demonstrated along the way are more important than getting to the next game level (or the final grade).

2

Encourage parents not to **"overhelp"** their children with assignments and projects so that the kids can wrestle with the content themselves. We want to see what the student can accomplish, not what the parents can.

CREATING A GROWTH MINDSET SCHOOL CULTURE

To work toward a growth mindset school culture is a commitment that all stakeholders must make. Be cognizant of new educators joining your staff and have a plan for getting them on board with your growth mindset goals. Continually monitor and reflect on practices that are having an impact and those that need to be improved upon:

1
Would visitors to your school pick up on the persistence and effort that your students are putting forth? Are more students embracing challenging tasks?

2
Are teachers using language that acknowledges what students do rather than who they are?

3
Are students using growth mindset language and talking about neural connections?

4
Are expectations high for all students?

5 Tips for a Growth Mindset School Culture

The commitment to building and maintaining a learning environment where expectations are high for all students and where all students value effort and perseverance is well worth the time. Adopting some of the components will incite some change, but in order to have the most impact, a symphony of the following should occur:

1. Educators should believe that all students can achieve and be successful.
2. Students should have a conceptual understanding of neural connections and believe that with effort and perseverance they can learn, be successful, and grow their intelligence.
3. Differentiated, responsive instruction should meets students where they are, giving them what they need, when they need it, and how they need it.
4. Critical thinking opportunities should be embedded in curriculum, instruction, and assessment for all students.
5. A broadened conception of **"giftedness"** should focus on talent development and domain-specific strengths, and rely heavily on the word **"potential"** rather than the word **"gifted."**

It is time to meet students where they are, expect the best from all of them, and provide opportunities for each and every student to succeed. A growth mindset school culture will open doors for all students.

Additional Resources

The following books provide more in-depth information about building a growth mindset learning community:

For Parents:
- *Mindsets for Parents: Strategies to Encourage Growth Mindsets in Kids* (2016) by Mary Cay Ricci and Margaret Lee (partner book with *Mindsets in the Classroom* that includes parent book club questions)

For Educators:
- *Mindsets in The Classroom: Building a Growth Mindset Learning Community* (2017) by Mary Cay Ricci
- *Ready-to-Use Resources for Mindsets in the Classroom* (2015) by Mary Cay Ricci

For Kids (Grades 3–7):
- *Nothing You Can't Do!: The Secret Power of Growth Mindsets* (2018) by Mary Cay Ricci

References

Dweck, C. (2006). *Mindset: The new psychology of success*: New York, NY: Random House.

Dweck, C. S. (2010). Mind-sets and equitable education. *Principal Leadership, 10*(5), 26–29.

Lohman, D. F. (2002, January 9). *Reasoning abilities*. Retrieved from http://faculty.education.uiowa.edu/docs/dlohman/rea soning_abilities.pdf

Ricci, M. C. (2017). *Mindsets in the classroom: Building a growth mindset learning community* (Rev. ed.). Waco, TX: Prufrock Press.

Ricci, M. C. (2015). *Ready-to-use resources for mindsets in the classroom: Everything educators need for building growth mindset learning communities*. Waco, TX: Prufrock Press.

Ricci, M. C., & Lee, M. (2016). *Mindsets for parents: Strategies to encourage growth mindsets in kids*. Waco, TX: Prufrock Press.

About the Author

Mary Cay Ricci has been an elementary and middle school teacher, a central office administrator, and an adjunct professor at Johns Hopkins University. She is the *New York Times* best-selling author of *Mindsets in the Classroom: Building a Growth Mindset Learning Community*. Follow her on Twitter @MaryCayR for more information and ideas about mindsets.

$12.95 US

PRUFROCK PRESS INC.™

ISBN-13: 978-1-61821-791-2

51295

9 781618 217912